The Guide for Hot Pot Cooking

Pot Cooking

The Best Hot Pot Cookbook That Will
Become Your Best Friend in The Kitchen

BY: Valeria Ray

License Notes

A Special Reward for Purchasing My Book!

Thank you, cherished reader, for purchasing my book and taking the time to read it. As a special reward for your decision, I would like to offer a gift of free and discounted books directly to your inbox. All you need to do is fill in the box below with your email address and name to start getting amazing offers in the comfort of your own home. You will never miss an offer because a reminder will be sent to you. Never miss a deal and get great deals without having to leave the house! Subscribe now and start saving!

https://valeria-ray.gr8.com

Contents

Delicious Hot Pot Recipes.. 7

Chapter I - Hot Pot Broths... 8

    (1) Vegetarian Broth 9

    (2) Sukiyaki Broth 11

    (3) Easy Chicken Broth 13

    (4) Soy Milk Broth.. 15

    (5) Superior Soup... 17

    (6) Kimchi Soup 19

    (7) Chicken Barbecue Broth 21

    (8) Laksa Soup 23

    (9) Spicy Sichuan Soup 25

    (10) Taiwanese-style Broth... 28

    (11) Satay Soup 30

    (12) Tom Yum Soup 33

(13) Classic Sichuan Broth 35

Chapter II - Hot Pot Ingredients 38

(14) Fish Cakes 39

(15) Fried Tofu Puffs 42

(16) Shrimp Balls 44

(17) Meatballs 47

(18) Pork Dumplings 49

Chapter III - Hot Pot Sauces 51

(19) Sesame Sauce 52

(20) Chili Padi Dipping Sauce 54

(21) Spicy Soy Vinegar Sauce 56

(22) Suki Dipping Sauce 58

(23) Mongolian Dipping Sauce 60

(24) Special Taiwanese Sauce 62

(25) Sacha Dipping Sauce 64

(26) Hot Pepper and Scallion Sauce 66

(27) Garlicky Dipping Sauce 68

(28) Gingered Scallion Sauce... 70

Chapter IV - Magical Hot Pot Recipes 72

(29) Spiced Chicken Hot Pot 73

(30) Mongolian-style Hot Pot 75

(31) Chinese-Style Hot Pot... 77

(32) Tasty Mongolian Hot Pot Bowls 80

(33) Spicy Lamb Hot Pot... 83

(34) Asian Hot Pot Bowls... 86

(35) Classic Sichuan Hot Pot 89

(36) Delightful Seafood Hot Pot.. 92

(37) Sukiyaki Hot Pot.. 94

About the Author.. 97

Author's Afterthoughts.. 99

Delicious Hot Pot Recipes

MMMMMMMMMMMMMMMMMMMMMMMMMMMMMMMMM

Chapter I - Hot Pot Broths

MMMMMMMMMMMMMMMMMMMMMMMMMMMMMMMM

(1) Vegetarian Broth

For those who like to derive the delicious difference from choice vegetables instead of meat or instant mixes, this is the broth recipe for you. It is healthy and delicious. But you would want to take your time simmering this concoction in order to extract the naturally sweet flavors of the veggies.

Serving Size: 12 cups

Cooking Time: 3 hrs 10 mins

List of Ingredients:

- 3 L water
- ½ lb. turnips, peeled and roughly sliced
- 2 cups carrots, peeled and roughly sliced
- 1 cup chestnuts
- 2 sprigs bamboo cane root

MMMMMMMMMMMMMMMMMMMMMMMMMMMMMMMM

Methods:

1. Bring the water to a boil in a stockpot over the high heat.

2. Add the rest of the ingredients and bring to a boil.

3. Turn the heat to low and simmer for 3 hours.

(2) Sukiyaki Broth

This Japanese-style hot pot broth is perfect for an all meat experience. It goes well with thin slices of beef, pork, and chicken plus noodles. It is sweet and savory and is pretty easy to make compared to other hot pot soups.

Serving Size: 16 cups

Cooking Time: 1 hr 10 mins

List of Ingredients:

- 3 L water
- 2 sachets Bonito soup base
- 2 pcs onions, sliced
- 2 pcs carrots, sliced
- 5 pcs dried Shiitake mushrooms, soaked and sliced
- 1 cup Tsuyu
- 1 cup Mirin

MMMMMMMMMMMMMMMMMMMMMMMMMMMMMMM

Methods:

1. Combine all the ingredients together in a stockpot.

2. Bring to a boil, then reduce to a simmer and cook for 30 minutes to an hour.

(3) Easy Chicken Broth

The plain and simple taste of chicken broth is a favorite for hot pot recipes. It is very easy to prepare and has a very basic taste that will mix well with any type of ingredient. Ideally, you would want your broth to be simple. The flavors will get stronger as it continues to simmer and as different ingredients are added to the broth.

Serving Size: 6 cups

Cooking Time: 5 mins

List of Ingredients:

- 6 cups water
- 1 pc chicken bouillon, crushed
- Pinch of ground black pepper
- 2 pcs scallions, sliced

MMMMMMMMMMMMMMMMMMMMMMMMMMMMMMMMM

Methods:

1. Heat water in a saucepan over medium heat.

2. Add the crushed chicken bouillon, stirring until dissolved.

3. Season with the ground pepper and sliced scallions before transferring to a hot pot.

(4) Soy Milk Broth

Soya is packed with umami flavor that is delightful any way you have it. If you use it as a soup base for your hot pot, you easily get that advantage to bathe your raw ingredients with. What's even more amazing about this soup recipe is that you get to enjoy it after only about 10 minutes of preparation.

Serving Size: 16 cups

Cooking Time: 10 mins

List of Ingredients:

- 1 L soy milk, unsweetened
- 1 L water
- 1 cup Sake
- 1 cup tablespoons mirin
- ½ teaspoons salt

MMMMMMMMMMMMMMMMMMMMMMMMMMMMMMMM

Methods:

1. Combine all the ingredients in a stockpot.

2. Boil for 10 minutes before transferring to a hot pot.

(5) Superior Soup

Pork and chicken combine delightfully well in this hot pot broth recipe. To get the best tasting, rich flavors of both, you will have to enjoy it after about 3 hours of continues simmering on low heat.

Serving Size: 16 cups

Cooking Time: 3 hrs 25 mins

List of Ingredients:

- 5 L water
- ½ pork chunks
- ½ lb. chicken chunks
- 2 lbs. pig's leg bone
- White pepper to taste

MMMMMMMMMMMMMMMMMMMMMMMMMMMMMMMMMM

Methods:

1. Boil water in a stockpot over high heat.

2. Add the pork, chicken, and pig's leg bone. Bring to a boil.

3. Remove the scum that floats to the surface.

4. Reduce the heat to low and continue cooking for the next 3 hours.

5. Season with white pepper before serving.

(6) Kimchi Soup

Delightfully Korean, this Kimchi inspired soup takes the flavor of the popular delicacy to create an enriching broth that will give a different color to your usual hot pot experience. There is so much to look forward to in this soup base: the nutty flavor of Kimchi, the spicy kick of Gochujang, and the umami taste of anchovies. What more can you ask for?

Serving Size: 12 cups

Cooking Time: 30 mins

List of Ingredients:

- 1 lb. Napa cabbage Kimchi
- 4 Tablespoons Gochujang
- 1 cup dried anchovies
- 2 L water
- 1 pc leek, thinly sliced
- 2 teaspoons garlic, minced
- 2 tablespoons Shaoxing wine
- 4 teaspoons sesame oil
- 1 tablespoon light soy sauce

MMMMMMMMMMMMMMMMMMMMMMMMMMMMMMMMMM

Methods:

5. Boil water in a stockpot over medium-high heat.

6. Add the anchovies and sliced leeks. Cook for 5 minutes.

7. Stir in the rest of the ingredients and cook for another 10 minutes or until fragrant.

(7) Chicken Barbecue Broth

Chicken stock is made more delightful with the addition of barbecue sauce in this hot pot broth version. With some added flavors, you will surely enjoy washing your ingredients in this mix, no matter what those may be. It has a slight hint of sweetness that helps balance out saltiness, providing additional umami into the meal.

Serving Size: 6 cups

Cooking Time: 10 mins

List of Ingredients:

- 6 cups chicken stock
- ½ cup barbecue sauce
- 2 teaspoons sugar
- ¼ cup fish sauce
- Pinch of Kosher salt
- Juice of 1 lime

MMMMMMMMMMMMMMMMMMMMMMMMMMMMMMMMMM

Methods:

1. Bring the chicken stock to a boil.

2. Once it starts to bubble, stir in the barbecue sauce and the rest of the ingredients.

3. Mix to dissolve the sugar and salt. Add more lime juice if you prefer to add some more sourness.

(8) Laksa Soup

This Singapore-inspired hot pot broth is rich and comforting. It's a great soup base to prepare whenever you are looking for something more exciting than the simple and basic chicken broth.

Serving Size: 16 cups

Cooking Time: 35 mins

List of Ingredients:

- 1.6 L water
- 2 cups Laksa paste
- 4 cups coconut milk
- 2 Tablespoons fish sauce

MMMMMMMMMMMMMMMMMMMMMMMMMMMMMMMMMMMM

Methods:

1. Combine all the ingredients in a stockpot. Cook at a simmer for 30 minutes or until fragrant, stirring occasionally.

(9) Spicy Sichuan Soup

From plain and simple to a spicy hot soup base. This Sichuan flavored spicy broth is a common choice in most parts of Asia, including Thailand, Korea, and China. It is a perfectly seasoned stock that would increasingly enhance the taste of any ingredient you dip into it.

Serving Size: 6 cups

Cooking Time: 25 mins

List of Ingredients:

- 6 cups vegetable stock
- 4 pcs dried Sichuan chilies
- 2 oz whole Sichuan peppercorns
- 2 pcs red chilies, seeded and sliced
- 1 tablespoon chili bean paste
- 1 tablespoon chili sauce
- 9 oz chili oil
- 6 pcs dried Chinese mushrooms
- 1 tablespoon fresh ginger, peeled and grated
- ¼ cup dried orange peel
- 2 pcs star anise
- 2 Tablespoons peanut oil

MMMMMMMMMMMMMMMMMMMMMMMMMMMMMMM

Methods:

1. Heat the peanut oil in a large saucepan over medium heat.

2. Add the Sichuan chilies and peppercorns, stirring frequently for a minute or until fragrant.

3. Whisk in chili bean paste and chili sauce, mixing until blended.

4. Stir in vegetable stock, mushrooms, orange peel, ginger, and chili oil.

5. Bring to a boil, then reduce heat to low and simmer for about 20 minutes until the flavors come together.

(10) Taiwanese-style Broth

There is something magical about the mix of different spices and ingredients in a stockpot. After giving them some time to simmer, you get the best-tasting base that could further enhance the flavors of your raw ingredients. This recipe is a proof of that.

Serving Size: 12 cups

Cooking Time: 1 hr

List of Ingredients:

- 3 L chicken stock
- 6 pcs Chinese red dates
- 2 Tablespoons Goji berries
- 10 pcs dried longans in shell
- 10 cloves garlic, peeled
- 2 Tablespoons spring onion, halved
- 2 Tablespoons ginger, peeled and grated
- 6 pcs Thai cardamom pods
- 6 pcs green cardamom pods
- 1 tablespoon nutmeg
- 2 pcs dried bay leaves
- 1 teaspoon cumin seeds
- 10 pcs dried chillies, sliced
- 1 tablespoon Sichuan peppercorns
- 1 tablespoon white peppercorns
- 1 tablespoon salt

MMMMMMMMMMMMMMMMMMMMMMMMMMMMMMMMM

Methods:

1. Place all the ingredients in a stockpot. Cook at a simmer for 1 hour.

(11) Satay Soup

Give your hot pot dinner a delightful crunch courtesy of this broth recipe that is accentuated with toasted peanuts ground to perfection. It is a nice base for fish cakes, raw fish fillets, and a variety of meats. You will even love to dip in fried tofu in this.

Serving Size: 8 cups

Cooking Time: 1 hr 10 mins

List of Ingredients:

- 1 ½ lb. peanuts, toasted and ground
- ½ cup dried shrimps
- 2 Tablespoons shrimp paste
- 8 cloves garlic, minced
- 2 pcs onions, chopped
- 8 cm galangal, smashed
- 2 stalks lemongrass, smashed
- 10 pcs dried chili, sliced
- 2 Tablespoons tamarind juice
- 1 L water
- 8 Tablespoons brown sugar
- 1 cup vegetable oil

MMMMMMMMMMMMMMMMMMMMMMMMMMMMMMMM

Methods:

1. Sauté garlic, onions, dried shrimp, shrimp paste, and dried chilies in oil over medium heat.

2. Add the lemongrass and galangal, stirring frequently until fragrant.

3. Stir in the peanuts, tamarind juice, sugar, and water.

4. Bring the mixture to a boil and simmer for 30 minutes until smooth and thick.

(12) Tom Yum Soup

This flavorful soup base features a unique aroma and spicy kick. It is light and versatile and would go pretty well not just with prawns, as most tom yum soups are made with, but also with thinly sliced meats. It's a great mixture of choice ingredients to wash your palates\ with.

Serving Size: 16 cups

Cooking Time: 30 mins

List of Ingredients:

- 4 Tablespoons Tom Yum paste
- 8 Cm Galangal root, smashed
- 2 tablespoons ginger, peeled and sliced
- 1 pcs shallot, sliced
- 2 stalks lemongrass, sliced
- 8 pcs lime leaves
- 4 pcs Thai red chilies
- 1 L water
- 1 L chicken stock
- 2 Tablespoons evaporated milk
- 4 Tablespoons fish sauce

MMMMMMMMMMMMMMMMMMMMMMMMMMMMMMMM

Methods:

1. Combine all of the ingredients in a stockpot, except for the Tom Yum paste, milk, and fish sauce. Bring to a boil.

2. Reduce heat to low before adding the remaining ingredients. Stir and cook for 20 minutes or until fragrant.

(13) Classic Sichuan Broth

There are two basic broths used in original Chinese hot pots: the classic chicken stock and the spicy Sichuan broth. This is the recipe that is commonly used for by those who like a little bit of spike for their hot pot. As with anything, you can adjust the level of spiciness of this soup base by controlling the amount of chilies and Sichuan peppercorns that you put in.

Serving Size: 16 cups

Cooking Time: 10 mins

List of Ingredients:

- 1 package spicy hot pot soup base
- 15 cups chicken stock
- 1 tablespoon Sichuan peppercorns
- 12 pcs whole dried red chilies
- 1 knob ginger, sliced
- 10 garlic cloves, peeled
- 1 pc cinnamon stick
- 10 pcs cloves
- 5 pcs star anise
- 4 pcs bay leaves
- 2 Tablespoons vegetable oil

MMMMMMMMMMMMMMMMMMMMMMMMMMMMMM

Methods:

1. Heat oil in a wok over medium heat.

2. Stir in the sliced ginger, mixing frequently for about 2 minutes or until fragrant.

3. Add the garlic cloves, cloves, bay leaves, star anise, and cinnamon stick.

4. Cook for another 2 minutes, stirring occasionally, before adding Sichuan peppercorns, chilies, and the contents of the hot pot soup base package.

5. Pour in the chicken stock and bring to a boil.

6. Divide into two hot pots when ready to use.

Chapter II - Hot Pot Ingredients

MMMMMMMMMMMMMMMMMMMMMMMMMMMMMMMMMMM

(14) Fish Cakes

n

Fish cakes are a delicacy on their own. They have that inimitable flavor brought about by the addition of potatoes, parsley, and butter into the grind. Naturally, you would have to fry the fish cake. But if you are using it for a hot pot, you can simply leave it as is and allow it to cook in simmering broth for a few minutes. Since it is fish, it will not take a long time to cook anyway.

Serving Size: 12 cakes

Cooking Time: 45 mins

List of Ingredients:

- 1 lb. cod fillets, cubed (you may substitute cod with salmon or whatever fish fillet you have available)
- 2 pcs potatoes, peeled and halved
- 1 tablespoon butter
- 1 tablespoon parsley, chopped
- 1 tablespoon onion, grated
- 1 pc egg, lightly beaten
- 3 Tablespoons vegetable oil

MMMMMMMMMMMMMMMMMMMMMMMMMMMMMMM

Methods:

1. Place potatoes in a stockpot. Cover with enough water and boil until tender or for about 15 minutes.

2. Add the fish fillet to the pot, cook for another 5 minutes. Drain and transfer to a mixing bowl.

3. Roughly mash boiled potatoes and fish. Add butter, parsley, egg, and onions. Mix until blended.

4. Form mixture into patties.

5. Fry fish cakes in vegetable oil until brown or refrigerate until ready to use.

(15) Fried Tofu Puffs

Tofu is a must-have at any hot pot dinner. You can serve it as is, sliced, or you can fry it to make interesting tofu puffs. If you fry this tofu fresh, they will have a nice, crispy texture and would surface instantly on your hot pot. If fried frozen, the center would be heavy enough, causing it to stay soaked in broth.

Serving Size: 2 cups

Cooking Time: 10 mins

List of Ingredients:

- 1 block firm tofu, drained on paper towels and cubed
- ¾ cup vegetable oil

MMMMMMMMMMMMMMMMMMMMMMMMMMMMMMMM

Methods:

1. Preheat oil in a wok on high.

2. When the oil is almost smoking, add the tofu cubes. Turn occasionally to brown on all sides.

(16) Shrimp Balls

Shrimp is a hot pot staple. It is often part of the raw seafood platter. It cooks easily and would only take about 2 minutes for a whole shrimp with head and tails to cook in a continuously simmering broth. Other times, shrimps are served in ball form, making it much easier to consume. FYI: A lot of people complain about the hard task of peeling shrimps when they are in a hot pot.

Serving Size: 24 balls

Cooking Time: 20 mins

List of Ingredients:

- 1 lb. shrimp, shelled and deveined
- 1 pc scallion, chopped
- 4 teaspoons cornstarch
- 1 pc egg white, beaten until frothy
- 1 teaspoon Shaoxing wine
- 1 teaspoon canola oil
- ¼ teaspoons Kosher salt
- ¼ teaspoons ground white pepper

MMMMMMMMMMMMMMMMMMMMMMMMMMMMMMM

Methods:

1. Pat the dry shelled and deveined shrimps using a paper towel.

2. Transfer the shrimp to a food processor, pulsing until finely minced.

3. Scrape the minced shrimps into a bowl.

4. Add the scallions, egg white, cornstarch, wine, and oil. Season with salt and pepper. Mix until well combined.

5. Form the mixture into balls, then arrange on a parchment paper lined baking tray. Refrigerate until ready to use.

(17) Meatballs

Another interesting tweak that you can add to your hot pot is a plate of meatballs. While it is common that you serve paper-thin slices of beef, chicken, pork, and lamb along with your hot pot soup, you can also go for a meatball recipe as simple as this one.

Serving Size: 50 meatballs

Cooking Time: 30 mins

List of Ingredients:

- 2 lbs. ground beef
- 2 pcs eggs, beaten
- 2 Tablespoons garlic, minced
- 1 cup dry parmesan cheese
- 1 cup Italian breadcrumbs
- 4 teaspoons Worcestershire sauce
- ½ teaspoons salt
- ¼ teaspoons pepper

MMMMMMMMMMMMMMMMMMMMMMMMMMMMMMMMMM

Methods:

1. Preheat the oven to 425 °F. Prepare a lightly greased baking sheet. Set aside.

2. Combine all of the ingredients in a mixing bowl. Hand mix until well blended.

3. Form into 2-inch balls and place on the prepared baking sheet.

4. Bake for 10 minutes until golden.

5. Allow them to cool on a wiring rack before serving.

(18) Pork Dumplings

A simple dumpling recipe is a great addition to a hot pot spread. Pork mince mixed with chives and ginger is definitely a good dish to start. You can prepare this ahead of time and store them in the freezer until you are ready to start a hot pot dinner.

Serving Size: 24 dumplings

Cooking Time: 40 mins

List of Ingredients:

- 24 pcs dumpling wrappers
- 1 lb. pork mince
- ½ cup Chinese chives, minced
- 1 tablespoon fresh ginger, grated
- 2 Tablespoons sherry cooking wine
- 2 teaspoons soy sauce
- ½ teaspoons kosher salt

MMMMMMMMMMMMMMMMMMMMMMMMMMMMMMM

Methods:

1. Combine all of the ingredients in a bowl except for the wrappers. Mix until well blended.

2. Spoon some filling onto the center of a dumpling wrapper. Fold in a half moon shape, pinching the edges to seal.

3. Store in the freezer until ready to use.

Chapter III - Hot Pot Sauces

MMMMMMMMMMMMMMMMMMMMMMMMMMMMMMMMM

(19) Sesame Sauce

The flavor of toasted sesame seeds is the star of this particular dipping sauce. It is great enough to provide some full-bodied flavor that will make everything, especially your shaved sheets of meat, extra delicious.

Serving Size: ½ cup

Cooking Time: 10 mins

List of Ingredients:

- ¼ cup sesame seeds, toasted
- 1 ½ teaspoons sesame oil
- ½ teaspoons ginger, peeled and roughly chopped
- 1 teaspoon peanut butter
- ¼ cup water
- 1 tablespoon rice vinegar
- 2 Tablespoons soy sauce
- ½ teaspoons sugar

MMMMMMMMMMMMMMMMMMMMMMMMMMMMMMMMM

Methods:

1. Place all the ingredients in a food processor. Pulse until puréed and smooth.

(20) Chili Padi Dipping Sauce

One of the simplest concoctions that you can create as your hot pot condiment, this chili padi dip is simply spicy with only a bit of lime juice and soy sauce. With its very basic taste, it will allow your hot pot ingredients to shine big time.

Serving Size: 1 cup

Cooking Time: 5 mins

List of Ingredients:

- 10 pcs bird's eyes chili (chili padi), sliced
- Juice of 3 limes
- 2 Tablespoons light soy sauce
- 1 teaspoon sesame oil
- 4 cloves garlic, peeled and minced

MMMMMMMMMMMMMMMMMMMMMMMMMMMMMMMM

Methods:

1. Whisk together the ingredients in a bowl until blended.

(21) Spicy Soy Vinegar Sauce

This is one of the simplest yet tastiest sauce concoctions that you can use as a dipping sauce for your hot pot. It only has three ingredients and takes less than 5 minutes to prepare.

Serving Size: ½ cup

Cooking Time: 3 mins

List of Ingredients:

- 2 pcs red chili, seeded and finely chopped
- 6 Tablespoons light soy sauce
- 6 Tablespoons balsamic vinegar

MMMMMMMMMMMMMMMMMMMMMMMMMMMMMMMMM

Methods:

1. Mix all of the ingredients in a bowl until well combined.

(22) Suki Dipping Sauce

This Thailand-style sauce is sweet and spicy with a bit of gooey consistency. It's an experience all on its own, starting with just this dipping sauce first. This goes perfectly well for Tom Yum soup based hot pot dinners.

Serving Size: 1 cup

Cooking Time: 10 mins

List of Ingredients:

- ½ cup red hot chilies, chopped
- 5 garlic cloves, chopped
- 1 tablespoon chopped coriander
- 1 tablespoon toasted sesame seeds
- 2 Tablespoons sweet chili sauce
- 2 Tablespoons ground bean sauce
- 2 Tablespoons fish sauce
- ½ Tablespoons lime juice
- ½ teaspoons sesame oil
- 2 Tablespoons water
- 1 tablespoon palm sugar, grated
- ½ teaspoons salt
- 1 teaspoon sugar

MMMMMMMMMMMMMMMMMMMMMMMMMMMMMMMM

Methods:

1. Combine all of the ingredients in a bowl, except for sesame seeds and coriander. Use them for garnish right before serving.

(23) Mongolian Dipping Sauce

The secret to a tasty hot pot experience is sometimes in the sauce. How rich and flavorful the sauce is can actually affect how much you enjoy the taste of your raw food dipped in simmering hot, flavored broth. This Mongolian-style dipping sauce is one of the best concoctions you can offer your guests around a hot pot. It's a bit spicy but definitely delicious.

Serving Size: 1 cup

Cooking Time: 12 minutes

List of Ingredients:

- 2 garlic cloves, minced
- 2 Tablespoons sesame oil
- 3 Tablespoons rice vinegar
- 2 teaspoons chili garlic sauce
- ¾ cup soy sauce
- 2 teaspoons sake
- 1 tablespoon dry sherry

MMMMMMMMMMMMMMMMMMMMMMMMMMMMMMM

Methods:

1. Whisk together all of the ingredients in a bowl. Cover and chill until ready to use.

(24) Special Taiwanese Sauce

As the word for the hot pot spread throughout Asia, different regions started to make their own versions. This Taiwanese sauce blend is one of the unique offerings that make it different when you have a hot pot in Taiwan.

Serving Size: ½ cup

Cooking Time: 5 mins

List of Ingredients:

- 1 tablespoon spring onions, finely sliced
- 2 Tablespoons fresh cilantro leaves, finely chopped
- 2 pcs egg yolk
- 2 Tablespoons Oriental barbecue sauce
- 2 Tablespoons light soy sauce

MMMMMMMMMMMMMMMMMMMMMMMMMMMMMMMMMMMMM

Methods:

1. Combine all the ingredients in a bowl, stirring to blend.

(25) Sacha Dipping Sauce

Sacha is Taiwan's answer to Thai's satay sauce. It is mostly made up of a flavorful explosion that is a bit fishy and salty. For this hot pot dipping sauce, you may also add some heat to make it more interesting.

Serving Size: ½ cup

Cooking Time: 5 mins

List of Ingredients:

- ¼ cup sacha sauce
- 1 tablespoon peanuts, toasted and crushed
- 1 tablespoon cilantro leaves, finely chopped
- 2 pcs hot peppers, finely chopped
- 1 tablespoon spring onions, finely chopped
- 1 tablespoon garlic, finely chopped
- 2 teaspoons sesame oil
- 2 Tablespoons rice vinegar
- 1 tablespoon soy sauce
- 1 teaspoon sugar

MMMMMMMMMMMMMMMMMMMMMMMMMMMMMMM

Methods:

1. Combine all of the ingredients in a bowl until well blended.

(26) Hot Pepper and Scallion Sauce

Spicy sauces help balance the mild taste of the broth. This tasty but extremely spicy blend is an ideal dipping sauce when you use a simple chicken broth for your hot pot.

Serving Size: 1 cup

Cooking Time: 7 mins

List of Ingredients:

- 2 pcs chili peppers, julienned
- 6 pcs scallions, julienned
- 2 Tablespoons ginger, julienned
- ¼ cup cilantro leaves, cut into 1-inch pieces
- 1 tablespoon rice vinegar
- 2 Tablespoons soy sauce
- 1 teaspoon hot chili oil
- 2 Tablespoons peanut oil

MMMMMMMMMMMMMMMMMMMMMMMMMMMMMMMM

Methods:

1. Combine the chili peppers, scallions, ginger, and cilantro leaves in a bowl. Set aside.

2. Heat the peanut oil in a pan over medium heat.

3. Pour hot oil into the bowl with the pepper mixture.

4. Stir in the remaining ingredients and let stand until the scallions, cilantro leaves, and peppers are wilted.

(27) Garlicky Dipping Sauce

Garlic is the main ingredient in this particular dipping sauce recipe. The nutty flavor is kept well balanced by the addition of sugar and lemon juice.

Serving Size: ½ cup

Cooking Time: 5 mins

List of Ingredients:

- 2 Tablespoons soy sauce
- 2 Tablespoons water
- ½ Tablespoons garlic, finely chopped
- 1 ½ Tablespoons lemon juice
- ½ teaspoons sugar

MMMMMMMMMMMMMMMMMMMMMMMMMMMMMMMM

Methods:

1. Mix all of the ingredients in a bowl until sugar is dissolved.

(28) Gingered Scallion Sauce

Both the flavor of ginger and scallions are highlighted in this dipping sauce to help equalize the taste of usual hot pot ingredients. There is that refreshing, slightly spicy feel to this sauce, making it the perfect partner to simple chicken or vegetable broth.

Serving Size: ½ cup

Cooking Time: 7 mins

List of Ingredients:

- ½ cup fresh ginger, minced
- 2 cups scallion, chopped
- ¼ cup peanut oil
- 1 tablespoon toasted sesame oil
- 1 teaspoon kosher salt
- ¼ teaspoons ground white pepper

MMMMMMMMMMMMMMMMMMMMMMMMMMMMMMMM

Methods:

1. Heat the peanut oil in a small saucepan over medium heat.

2. Add the ginger, stirring for about a minute or until fragrant.

3. Stir in the scallions. Cook until wilted.

4. Turn off the heat, then season with toasted sesame oil, salt, and pepper.

Chapter IV - Magical Hot Pot Recipes

MMMMMMMMMMMMMMMMMMMMMMMMMMMMMMMMMM

(29) Spiced Chicken Hot Pot

Chicken is a favorite hot pot ingredient. In this recipe, delightful spiced chicken parts will help add some color to classic Sichuan broth. The meaty and rich taste is definitely comforting, especially during the cold winter days.

Serving Size: 4

Cooking Time: 10 mins

List of Ingredients:

- 8 cups Classic Sichuan Broth
- 1 lb. boneless chicken, cubed
- 8 oz Shiitake mushrooms, stems removed
- 1 cup Enoki mushrooms, rinsed and separated
- ½ cup green onions, chopped
- ½ cup Sesame Sauce
- ½ Garlicky Dipping Sauce

MMMMMMMMMMMMMMMMMMMMMMMMMMMMMMMMMMM

Methods:

1. Place ingredients in serving platters.

2. Serve together with simmering hot pot of Sichuan broth and the sauces.

(30) Mongolian-style Hot Pot

Unlike the other combinations, this recipe calls for the simplest ingredients. Some clear broth, thin slices of lamb, cubed soft tofu, and baby bok choy are already enough to make a tableful of delights. This is a wonderful recipe that's hearty and comforting and tasty in its own right.

Serving Size: 4

Cooking Time: 10 mins

List of Ingredients:

- 8 cups Easy Chicken Broth
- 1 lb. lamb, thinly sliced
- 1 block soft tofu, cubed
- 1 lb. baby bok choy, separated
- 4 oz cellophane noodles, soaked
- ½ cup Sesame Sauce

MMMMMMMMMMMMMMMMMMMMMMMMMMMMMMMMM

Methods:

1. Simmer broth in a hot pot. Serve with a platter of ingredients together with a sesame dipping sauce.

(31) Chinese-Style Hot Pot

From the country that started it all, this hot pot recipe is as authentic as authentic can get. This Chinese-inspired dish picks up the basic principles, using a simple and plain broth, shrimp balls, choice fresh ingredients, tofu, noodles, and two different sauce mixes.

Serving Size: 6

Cooking Time: 20 mins

List of Ingredients:

- 12 cups Chicken Barbecue Broth
- 24 pcs Shrimp Balls
- 1 cup raw beef sirloin, thinly sliced
- 1 bunch baby bok choy
- 1 cup Chinese cabbage, cut into 1-inch slices
- 1 cup baby corn
- 1 cup tofu, diced
- 9 oz thin rice noodles, prepared according to package instructions
- ½ cup vegetable oil
- ½ cup Gingered Scallion Sauce
- ½ cup Hot Pepper and Scallion Sauce

MMMMMMMMMMMMMMMMMMMMMMMMMMMMMMM

Methods:

1. Heat oil in a pan over medium heat.

2. Fry ½ cup of tofu, leaving the other half raw, until brown on all sides.

3. Arrange your hot pot ingredients in separate bowls or on a platter.

4. Serve around a simmering pot of broth with condiments on the side.

(32) Tasty Mongolian Hot Pot Bowls

Hot pot in a bowl is a common practice in some regions. No, it's not that they do not have a hot pot or table space big enough to spread out the ingredients. It's just that they want to enjoy the same goodness without going through the entire procedure in full length. This Mongolian hot pot is an example and a very tasty one.

Serving Size: 6

Cooking Time: 2 hrs 55 mins

List of Ingredients:

- 8 oz flank steak, sliced thinly
- 4 oz buckwheat noodles, uncooked
- 7 cups bok choy, thinly sliced
- 1 cup shiitake mushrooms, thinly sliced
- 1 cup carrots, sliced
- ½ cup green onions, thinly sliced
- 2 ½ Tablespoons fresh ginger, peeled and grated
- 2 cloves garlic, minced
- ¼ teaspoons red pepper, crushed
- 2 Tablespoons light soy sauce
- 2 Tablespoons hoisin sauce
- 1 ½ teaspoons dark sesame oil
- 2 14oz cans low-sodium beef broth
- 2 cups hot water
- 1 tablespoon rice vinegar
- Cooking spray

MMMMMMMMMMMMMMMMMMMMMMMMMMMMMMMMM

Methods:

1. Place flank steak slices in a Ziploc bag. Add ginger, garlic, crushed pepper, and soy sauce. Chill for 2 hours and 30 minutes, turning bag occasionally to coat the steak.

2. Heat a stockpot on high. Coat lightly with cooking spray and brown the beef, stirring frequently for about a minute or two. Transfer beef to a plate and set aside.

3. Add the bok choy, carrots, green onions, and mushrooms to the same pan. Stir-fry for 2 minutes.

4. Whisk in hoisin sauce, beef broth, and hot water. Let it boil.

5. Turn heat down to medium-low, add soba noodles, and cook for 5 minutes.

6. When noodles are done, add rice the vinegar and browned beef.

7. Serve in individual bowls. Drizzle each with dark sesame oil.

(33) Spicy Lamb Hot Pot

If you favor lamb among other types of meat and you are a fan of spicy broths, this is the perfect hot pot recipe for you. All the prepared ingredients, raw and cooked will surely blend well with the prepared Spicy Sichuan Soup. It is tasty with a nice level of heat. A must-try!

Serving Size: 6

Cooking Time: 20 mins

List of Ingredients:

- 12 cups Spicy Sichuan Soup
- 1 cup raw lamb, thinly sliced
- 2 cups raw prawns, shelled and deveined
- 9 oz fish balls
- 1 cup firm tofu, cut into chunks
- 1 cup tofu, diced and fried
- 1 cup Enoki mushrooms
- 2 cups baby corn
- 1 bunch Chinese cabbage, sliced
- 2 Tablespoons spring onions, coarsely chopped
- ½ cup Spicy Soy Vinegar Sauce
- ½ cup Special Taiwanese Sauce

MMMMMMMMMMMMMMMMMMMMMMMMMMMMMM

Methods:

1. Arrange all of the ingredients around a simmering pot of spicy soup.

2. Let your guests cook their choice of ingredients in the broth.

3. Place dipping sauces in small platters and serve on the side of individual plates.

(34) Asian Hot Pot Bowls

If you do not have much space to go through the entire hot pot ceremony, you can always fast-track the process. This is one of the most delightful ways to enjoy the principle behind the hot pot minus the mess and big-time preparation rituals.

Serving Size: 4

Cooking Time: 60 mins

List of Ingredients:

- 1 3.75oz package thin rice noodles, prepared according to package directions
- 4 pcs carrots, peeled and thinly sliced
- 8 oz green beans, cut into 2-inch pieces
- 8 oz shiitake mushrooms, thinly sliced
- 2 Tablespoons fresh ginger, grated
- 4 pcs scallions, thinly sliced
- 6 cups low-sodium chicken broth
- 2/3 cup light soy sauce
- 1 teaspoon chili sauce
- 1 tablespoon olive oil

MMMMMMMMMMMMMMMMMMMMMMMMMMMMMMM

Methods:

1. Stir-fry the mushrooms in olive oil over medium-high heat for about 2 minutes.

2. Add ginger, soy sauce, chili sauce, and broth. Bring to a boil.

3. Stir in the carrots, green beans, and scallions. Simmer for another 5 minutes or until the vegetables are tender.

4. Place noodles in four individual bowls.

5. Ladle soup with vegetables and serve immediately.

(35) Classic Sichuan Hot Pot

As far as the Chinese hot pot makers are concerned, there are two basic recipes to follow. First, there is the classic hot pot, Chinese style, characterized by a simple stock and a couple of choice ingredients. Then, there is the interestingly spicy Sichuan hot pot, characterized by chilies and Sichuan laden broth, making the bland, raw ingredients taste so good.

Serving Size: 8-12

Cooking Time: 1 hr

List of Ingredients:

- 12 cups Classic Sichuan Broth
- 2 cups beef, thinly shaved
- 2 cups chicken breast, deboned and sliced
- 12 pcs Classic Pork Dumplings
- 2 cups assorted fish balls
- 2 cups sea bass fillets, thinly sliced
- 2 cups firm tofu, sliced
- 1 cup fried tofu puffs
- 1 cup Shiitake mushrooms, stems removed and sliced
- 1 cup straw mushrooms, rinsed
- 1 cup wood ear mushrooms, sliced
- 1 cup mung bean vermicelli, soaked
- 1 cup fresh noodles
- 1 head green leaf lettuce
- 1 bunch bok choy
- 1 head Napa cabbage, sliced
- ½ cup Hot Pepper and Scallion Sauce

MMMMMMMMMMMMMMMMMMMMMMMMMMMMMMM

Methods:

1. Assemble the hot pot by first placing the broth in a fondue pot or whatever is available. Bring to a low boil.

2. Arrange all of the ingredients on serving plates gathered around the simmering broth.

3. Place the sauce in separate small bowls.

(36) Delightful Seafood Hot Pot

One of the best things about hot pots is that you can choose whichever ingredients you might like. You can easily concentrate on meats or meats and veggies, and in this recipe, seafood. Feel free to add a platter of thinly sliced meat for those who won't be very pleased without it.

Serving Size: 6

Cooking Time: 30 mins

List of Ingredients:

- 10 cups Superior Soup
- 8 pcs sea scallops, sliced
- 8 shucked oysters
- 4 pcs squid, cut into rings
- 12 pcs shrimp, peeled and deveined
- 1 16oz package soft tofu, drained and cubed
- 4 oz of dried bean thread noodles, soaked, then cut into bite-size pieces
- 1 lb. leafy greens, chopped into bite-size pieces
- ½ cup Garlicky Dipping Sauce
- ½ cup Gingered Scallion Sauce

MMMMMMMMMMMMMMMMMMMMMMMMMMMMMMMMMM

Methods:

1. Arrange all of the ingredients in a serving platter. Place around simmering broth together with the sauces.

(37) Sukiyaki Hot Pot

One of the most popular hot pot recipes in Japan is beef sukiyaki, characterized by a sukiyaki broth, very thin slices of strip loin, and a number of ingredients that are sure to make comforting bowls afterward. There are mushrooms, greens, tofu, and noodles to dip into the delightful broth.

Serving Size: 4

Cooking Time: 15 mins

List of Ingredients:

- 8 cups Sukiyaki broth
- 1 tablespoon beef fat trimmings
- 1 lb. beef strip loin, sliced paper-thin
- 6 oz firm tofu, cut into cubes
- ½ lb. napa cabbage, sliced
- 1 cup Arugula leaves, rinsed
- 10 pcs shallots, sliced
- 4 pcs Japanese leeks, sliced diagonally
- 7 oz Enoki mushrooms, trimmed and separated
- 4 oz Shiitake mushrooms, stems removed
- 7 oz Konnyaku noodles, rinsed, strained and roughly chopped
- ½ cup Spicy Soy Vinegar Sauce
- ½ cup Hot Pepper and Scallion Sauce

MMMMMMMMMMMMMMMMMMMMMMMMMMMMMM

Methods:

1. Heat beef trimmings in a nonstick pan over medium heat. Render fat for 2 minutes.

2. Add the beef slices and brown on both sides. Transfer to a plate.

3. Arrange all the remaining ingredients in separate plates. Serve with a simmering broth together with Spicy Soy Vinegar, Hot Pepper, and Scallion sauces.

About the Author

A native of Indianapolis, Indiana, Valeria Ray found her passion for cooking while she was studying English Literature at Oakland City University. She decided to try a cooking course with her friends and the experience changed her forever. She enrolled at the Art Institute of Indiana which offered extensive courses in the culinary Arts. Once Ray dipped her toe in the cooking world, she never looked back.

When Valeria graduated, she worked in French restaurants in the Indianapolis area until she became the head chef at one of the 5-star establishments in the area. Valeria's attention to taste and visual detail caught the eye of a local business person who expressed an interest in publishing her recipes. Valeria began her secondary career authoring cookbooks and e-books which she tackled with as much talent and gusto as her first career. Her passion for food leaps off the page of her books which have colourful anecdotes and stunning pictures of dishes she has prepared herself.

Valeria Ray lives in Indianapolis with her husband of 15 years, Tom, her daughter, Isobel and their loveable Golden Retriever, Goldy. Valeria enjoys cooking special dishes in her large, comfortable kitchen where the family gets involved in preparing meals. This successful, dynamic chef is an inspiration to culinary students and novice cooks everywhere.

$$\bullet\bullet\bullet\bullet\bullet\bullet\bullet\bullet\bullet\bullet\bullet\bullet\bullet\bullet\bullet\bullet\bullet\bullet$$

Author's Afterthoughts

Thank you for Purchasing my book and taking the time to read it from front to back. I am always grateful when a reader chooses my work and I hope you enjoyed it!

With the vast selection available online, I am touched that you chose to be purchasing my work and take valuable time out of your life to read it. My hope is that you feel you made the right decision.

I very much would like to know what you thought of the book. Please take the time to write an honest and informative review on Amazon.com. Your experience and opinions will be of great benefit to me and those readers looking to make an informed choice.

With much thanks,

Valeria Ray

Made in the USA
San Bernardino, CA
29 January 2020